G. THALBEN-BALL

LAUDATE DOMINUM

A COLLECTION
OF INTROITS

BOOK II

NOVELLO

CONTENTS

INTROITS

BOOK II

GEORGE THALBEN-BALL

1

Seek ye first God's King-dom and his righ-teous-ness.

2

Bless-ed are the pure in heart, for they shall see God. Bless-ed, bless-ed are the poor in spi-rit, for theirs is the King-dom of heav'n.

rall.

2

3

♩ = 90
mf

He that do - eth the will of God a -

bid - eth for ev - er, for ev - - er.

p dim. **rall.**

4

♩ = 100
p

Teach me to do the thing that pleas - eth___ thee; for thou___ art my God.

pp

5

♩ = 120
p

Bless the Lord, O my soul, and for - get not all___ his ben - i - fits.

6

♩ = 70
p

Eve - ry day will I___ give thanks un - to thee:___ and

will I give

praise__ thy Name__ for ev - er and ev - - er - more.

To S. R.

7

♩ = 80

Un - to thee,__ O Lord,__ do I__ lift

up__ my soul:__ my God,__ I trust__ in thee.

To S. S. W.

8

♩ = 88

Make me a clean heart, O God:__ and re -

new a right__ spi - rit with - in me.

9

♩ = 72

They— that wait— up - on the Lord— shall re-

new their— strength, shall re - new— their— strength.

To C. W.

10

♩ = 66

Com-fort, O Lord,— the soul of thy ser-vant: for un-to thee do I

lift— up my soul,— un-to thee— do I lift— up my soul.—

dim.

11

♩ = 104

If an - y man love me, he will keep my word: and my

5

Fa-ther will love him, and we will come un-to him and dwell with him.

12

Hold thee still in the Lord: and a-bide pa-tient-ly up - on him.

13

Heav'n and earth shall pass a - way, but

my word shall not pass a - way.

14

Be still, and know that I am God.

6

15

♩ = 72

mf _____ p

I am the light of___ the world. He that fol-low-eth me shall not walk in

dark - ness, but shall have the light_____ of___ life.

16

♩ = 88

p

God is light, and in him is no___ dark-ness at all.

17

♩ = 64

p

Je - sus said, Come un-to me all ye that la - bour

and are hea-vy la - den, and I will give_____ you rest.

18

I am the good Shep-herd; the good shep-herd lay-eth down his
life for the sheep. They shall be one flock, and one shep-herd.—

19

God is love: and he— that dwell-eth in love dwell-eth in God and God in him.

20

Quite free in time

Be ye fol-low-ers of God, and walk in
love: ev-en as Christ lov'd— us, and gave him-self— for us.

8

21

♩ = 104

O come, let us wor - ship and bow down: let us kneel be - fore the Lord our Mak - er, for he is our God.

22

♩ = 116

The Lord is in his ho - ly tem - ple:

dim. **rall.**

let all the earth keep si - lence be - fore him.

23

Freely

In the world ye shall have tri - bu - la - tion: but

be of good cheer; I have o - ver-come the___ world.

24

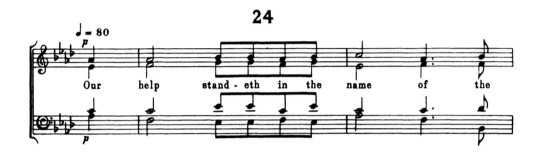

Our help stand-eth in the name of the

Lord, who hath made___ heav'n___ and___ earth.

25

Je-sus said, A - bide___ in me,___ and I in you.

26

This is life e-ter-nal, that they may know thee, and Je-sus Christ whom thou hast sent.

10

27

Rest in the Lord and wait pa-tient-ly on him and he shall give thee thy hearts de - sire.

28

We lift them up un - to the Lord.

We lift them up un - to the Lord.

We lift them up un - to the Lord.

Lift up your hearts. We lift them up un - to the Lord.

29

My soul, wait thou on - ly up - on

God;— for my ex - pec - ta - tion_ is from Him a - lone.

30

Be - hold I bring you good tid - ings of great joy which shall

be to all peo - ple. For un - to you_ is born in the

ci - ty of Da - vid a Sa - viour. which is Christ the Lord._

31

Happily

Al - le-lu - ia, Al - le-lu - ia, Al - le-lu - ia.

Un-to us a child is born. Al - le-lu - ia.

O come let us a - dore him.

Al - le-lu - ia, Al - le-lu - ia, Al - le - lu - ia.

dim.

pp

dim. **pp**

32

Maestoso Allegro

The Lord is ri - sen. He is ri - sen in-deed. Al - le-lu - ia,

cresc. *allarg.*

Al - le-lu - ia, Al - le-lu - ia, Al - le-lu - ia.

cresc.

33

14

lu - ia, Al - le - lu - ia.

34

Swiftly with animation

The Lord hath ma - ni - fe - sted forth his glo - ry. O

come,___ O come___ let us___ a - dore him, and

rall.

praise___ his name for e - ver. A - men.

Published by Novello Publishers Limited
Distributed by Music Sales Limited, Newmarket Road, Bury St. Edmunds, Suffolk IP33 3YB